Johann Sebastian Bach

THE WELL-TEMPERED CLAVIER

Books I and II, Complete

Dover Publications, Inc.
New York

This Dover edition, first published in 1983, contains all the music from Volume 14 (the 3rd volume of *Clavierwerke*), *Das Wohltemperirte Clavier,* 1866, of *Johann Sebastian Bach's Werke,* originally published by the Bach-Gesellschaft, Leipzig. The present volume includes corrections, tempo indications and an explanation of ornaments prepared specially by Professor Saul Novack of Queens University.

Manufactured in the United States of America
Dover Publications, Inc., 31 East 2nd Street, Mineola, N.Y. 11501

Library of Congress Cataloging in Publication Data

Bach, Johann Sebastian, 1685–1750.
[Wohltemperierte Klavier]
The well-tempered clavier.

For harpsichord.
Reprint. Originally published: Leipzig : Bach-Gesellschaft, 1866. (Johann Sebastian Bachs Werke ; Jahrg. 14) With corrections and explanation of ornaments by Saul Novack. 1. Harpsichord music. 2. Canons, fugues, etc. (Harpsichord) I. Novack, Saul. II. Title.
M22.B11W656 1983 83-5152
ISBN 0-486-24532-2

Contents

Das wohltemperirte Clavier,
oder Praeludia, und Fugen durch alle Tone und Semitonia
[The Well-Tempered Clavier,
or Preludes and Fugues in All Major and Minor Keys]

Book Two (1738–1742 [some pieces earlier]; BWV 870–893)

Note on Corrections

A number of minor alterations have been made silently in the text of the music to conform with some of the critical evaluations of the variant autograph manuscripts made by other scholars subsequent to the original publication of the Bach-Gesellschaft edition.

It should be noted that in this edition, in the treble clef, key signatures that include the sharping of F place the sharp sign in the lower position of F on the staff.

Note on Tempos

Bach did not provide tempo indications for all of the preludes and fugues in *The Well-Tempered Clavier,* and the original editor of the Bach-Gesellschaft edition (reprinted here) refrained from providing tempos. It is best to base the tempo of any prelude or fugue on the stylistic norms of the practice of Bach's day, and on the inherent rhythmic-melodic character of each unit. For didactic purposes, however, and for the guidance of less experienced players, the present Dover edition provides, in small type at the beginning of each prelude and each fugue, the tempo indications (including metronomic measure) suggested by Hans Bischoff in his prestigious edition. Furthermore, wherever the tempo indications given by the great scholar Donald F. Tovey differ from those of Bischoff, they have been added in parentheses in the form "(Tovey: . . .)"; we omit, however, Tovey's subjective suggestions for expression, such as "dolce ma espressivo" (Book Two, Prelude 20).

Note on Ornamentation

No alteration of ornaments as they appear in the Bach-Gesellschaft Edition have been made in this reprinting in view of the many variants in the various manuscript sources.

The following general principles are suggested: (1) Ornaments begin on the beat. (2) Whenever possible, the beginning of the ornament does not repeat the preceding note. (3) The ornament always moves downward, except in a variant of the trill, as shown below.

The Grace Note. The grace note (♪ or ♩) is in smaller print. It is the basic appoggiatura. Generally, its value is very short. A longer value is given, however, if it is attached to a note whose value is long. The shortest value appears in the form 𝅘𝅥𝅯.

The Trill. The trill is sustained, generally, for the duration of the value of the note to which it is applied, except in the case of the short trill, as shown below. The four forms of the trill, as they appear in this edition, are as follows:

THE WELL-TEMPERED CLAVIER
Book One

Prelude 1, C Major

25
30
35
Fugue 1, C Major
Andante ♩ = 63
a 4.
5
Oder:

Oder:
10
15
20
25

Prelude 2, C Minor

20
25
Presto
30
Adagio
Allegro
35

Fugue 2, C Minor

20
25
30

Prelude 3, C-sharp Major

55
60
65
70
75
80
85
90
95
100

Fugue 3, C-sharp Major

Prelude 4, C-sharp Minor

20
25
30
35

Fugue 4, C-sharp Minor

Molto moderato ♩ = 100
(Tovey: similar; maestoso)

65
70
75
80
85
90
95
100
105
110
115

Prelude 5, D Major

20
25
30
35

Fugue 5, D Major

Allegro moderato ♩ = 80
(Tovey: slower; in French overture style)

a 4.

15
20
25

Prelude 6, D Minor

15
20
Oder:
25

Fugue 6, D Minor

Moderato ♩ = 72 *(Tovey: similar)*

Prelude 7, E-flat Major

25
30
Oder:
35

40
45
50

Fugue 7, E-flat Major

Prelude 8, E-flat Minor

Fugue 8, D-sharp Minor

Andante ♩ = 72 *(Tovey: somewhat faster)*

45
50
55
60
65
70
75
80
85

Prelude 9, E Major

Allegretto piacevole ♩ = 92 *(Tovey: similar)*

Fugue 9, E Major

Prelude 10, E Minor

Presto

Fugue 10, E Minor

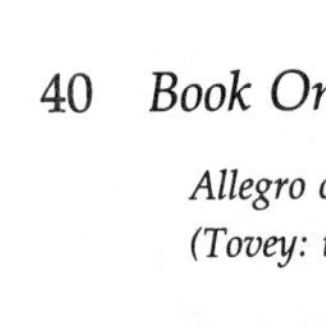

Allegro capriccioso ♩ = 132
(Tovey: the same; leggiero)

Oder:
20
25
30
35
40

Prelude 11, F Major

Fugue 11, F Major

Prelude 12, F Minor

15
20

Fugue 12, F Minor

Molto moderato ♩ = 66
(Tovey: similar; maestoso)

a 4.

Oder:
35
Oder:
40
45
50
55

Prelude 13, F-sharp Major

Allegretto ♪. = 104 *(Tovey: similar)*

Fugue 13, F-sharp Major

Andantino ♩ = 76 *(Tovey: similar)*

Prelude 14, F-sharp Minor

Allegro ♩ = 108

Fugue 14, F-sharp Minor

Andante serioso ♩ = 100
(Tovey: the same; cantabile)

Prelude 15, G Major

Fugue 15, G Major

Prelude 16, G Minor

Fugue 16, G Minor

Prelude 17, A-flat Major

25
30
35
40

Fugue 17, A-flat Major

20
25
30
35

Prelude 18, G-sharp Minor

Fugue 18, G-sharp Minor

Prelude 19, A Major

Allegretto grazioso ♩ = 84 *(Tovey: similar)*

15
20

Fugue 19, A Major

35
40
45
Oder:
50
Oder:

Prelude 20, A Minor

Allegro ♩. = 80 (*Tovey: slightly slower*)

Fugue 20, A Minor

Moderato assai ♩ = 66

30
35
40
45
50
tr
tr
(tr)
(tr)
55

Oder:

Prelude 21, B-flat Major

Vivace ♩ = 76 *(Tovey: in toccata style; improvisatory)*

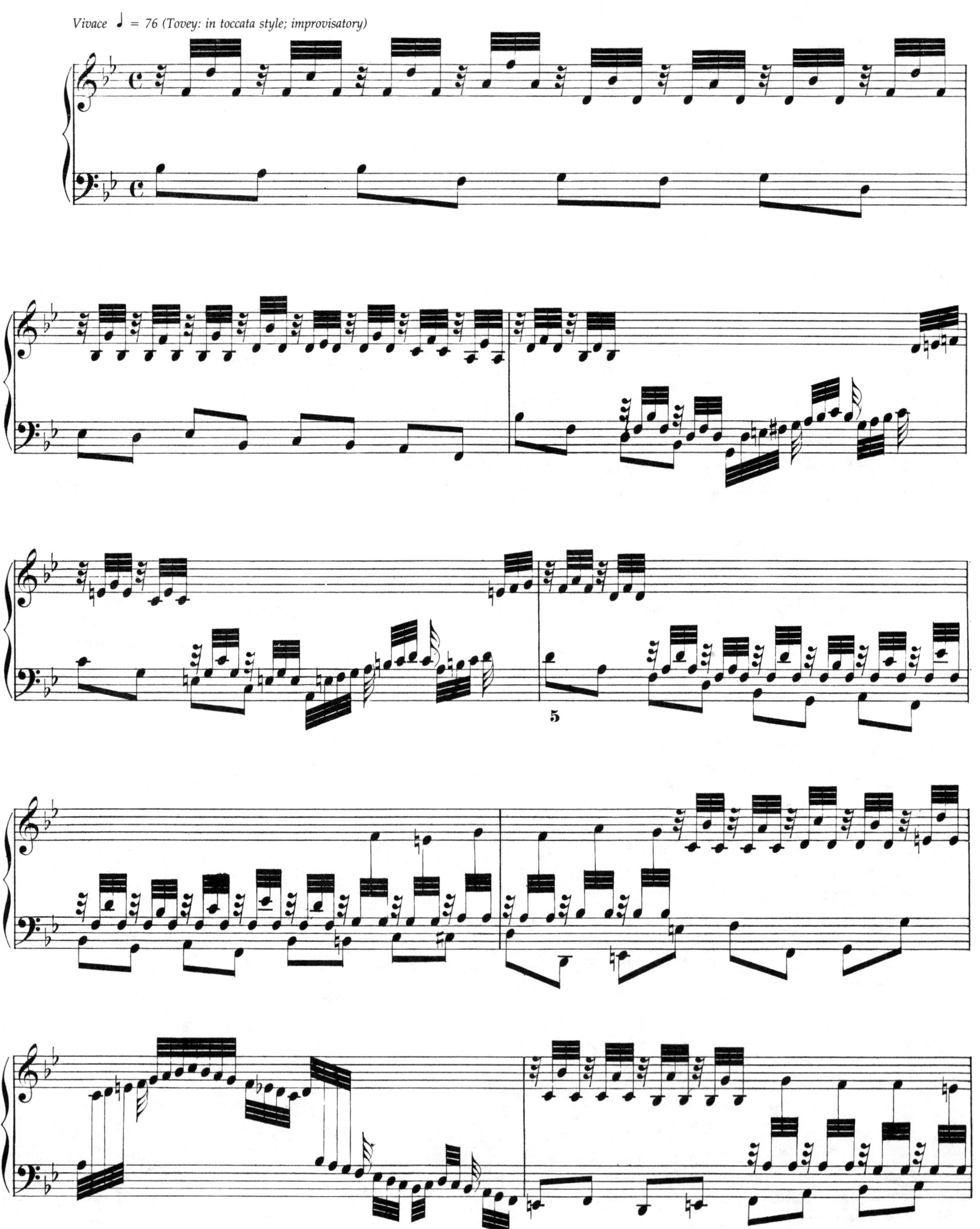

10
15
20

Fugue 21, B-flat Major

Allegro scherzando ♩ = 120 (Tovey: similar)

Prelude 22, B-flat Minor

15
20

Fugue 22, B-flat Minor

Lento ♩ = 104 *(Tovey: somewhat faster)*

Prelude 23, B Major

10
15
20
25
30

Prelude 24, B Minor

45
Largo ♩ = 52
Fugue 24, B Minor
a 4.
Largo.
tr
5
10
15
20

25
30
35

40
45
50
55

60
65
70
75

THE WELL-TEMPERED CLAVIER
Book Two

Prelude 1, C Major

Andante espressivo ♩ = 54 (Tovey: similar)

10
15
20

25
30

Fugue 1, C Major

Vivace ♩ = 112
a 3.
5

10

15

20
25

tr
30

35
tr
40

45
50
55
60
65
70
75
80

Prelude 2, C Minor

tr
tr
15
20
25

Fugue 2, C Minor

Molto tranquillo ♩ = 56 *(Tovey: similar)*

15
Oder:
20
25
Oder:

Prelude 3, C-sharp Major

*Throughout this prelude, the alternate versions (printed here in smaller type, and preceded by "Oder:") are now the preferred readings, on the basis of the best manuscript copies by Bach's pupils and the evaluations of later scholars, especially Bischoff and Tovey.

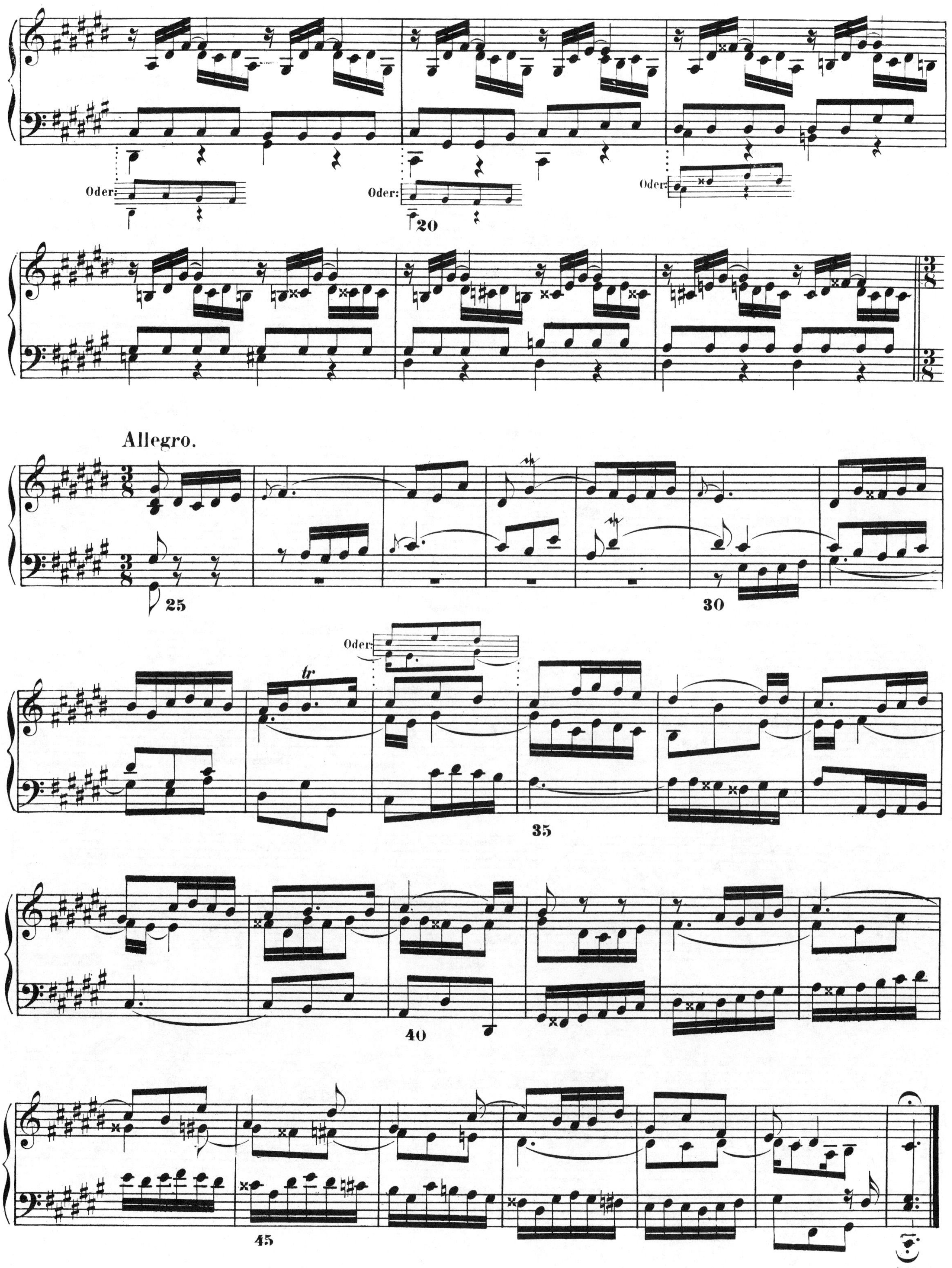
Oder:
Oder:
20
Oder:
Allegro.
25
30
Oder:
tr
35
40
45
50

Fugue 3, C-sharp Major

Moderato ♩ = 60 *(Tovey: somewhat similar)*

a 3.

10

15

Oder:

Oder:
20
Oder:
25
30
35

Prelude 4, C-sharp Minor

Oder:
Oder:
35
40
45
Oder:
50
55
Oder:
60

Fugue 4, C-sharp Minor

Vivace ♪ = 126 *(Tovey: slightly slower)*

a 3.

5

10

15

20

25

Oder:

30

40
45
50
Oder:
55
60
tr
65
70

Prelude 5, D Major

25
30
35
Oder:
tr
40

Fugue 5, D Major

Oder:

Prelude 6, D Minor

35
40
45
50
55
60

Fugue 6, D Minor

Moderato ♩ = 72 *(Tovey: similar)*

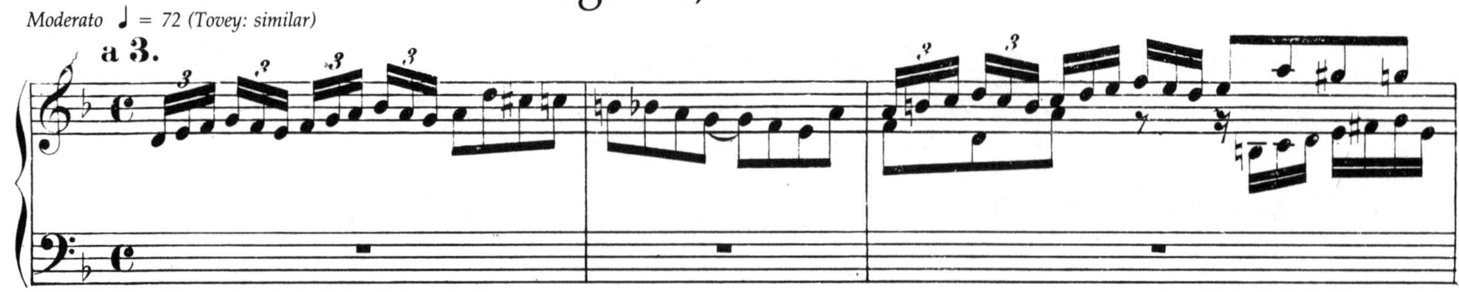

tr
15
20
25

Prelude 7, E-flat Major

Allegretto grazioso ♩. = 84

40
45
50
55
60
65
70

Fugue 7, E-flat Major

Moderato ♩ = 63

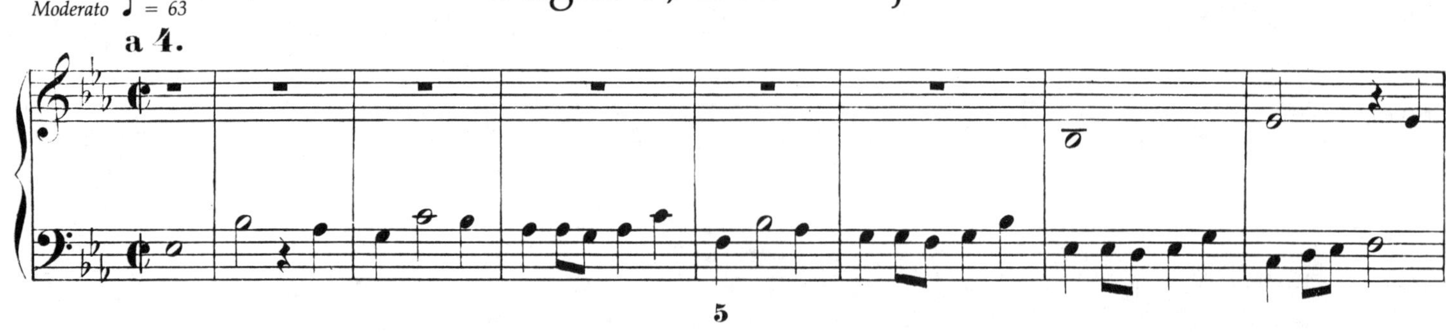

40
45
50
55
60
65
70

Prelude 8, D-sharp Minor

20
25
30
35

Fugue 8, D-sharp Minor

25
30
Oder:
Oder:
35
40
45

Prelude 9, E Major

30
35
40
45
Oder:
50

Fugue 9, E Major

Grave 𝅗𝅥 = 60 *(Tovey: similar)*

a 4.

5

10

*Preferred, in accordance with some manuscripts.

25
30
35
40

Prelude 10, E Minor

Oder:

Oder:

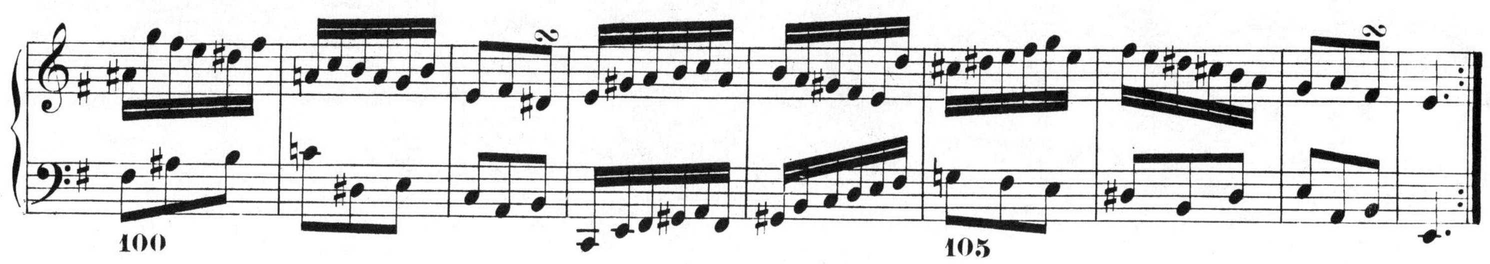

Fugue 10, E Minor

25
Oder:
30
Oder:
35

40
45
50
Oder:
55
60
Oder:

65
Oder:
70
75
80
85

Prelude 11, F Major

40
45
50
55
60
65
70

Fugue 11, F Major

55
60
65
70
75
80
85
90
95

Prelude 12, F Minor

Fugue 12, F Minor

Oder:
45
50
55
60
65
70
75
80
85

Prelude 13, F-sharp Major

Allegretto ♩ = 88 *(Tovey: similar)*

Oder:

tr
40
45
50
55
60
65
70
75

Fugue 13, F-sharp Major

Allegro 𝅗𝅥 = 69 *(Tovey: similar; in gavotte style)*

45
50
55
60
65
70
75
80
tr

Prelude 14, F-sharp Minor

Oder:
Oder:

Fugue 14, F-sharp Minor

Moderato ♩ = 72 (*Tovey: similar*)

45
50
55
60
65
70

Prelude 15, G Major

25
30
35
40
45

Fugue 15, G Major

40
45
tr
50
tr
Oder:
55
tr
tr
60
tr
65
70

Prelude 16, G Minor

15
20

Fugue 16, G Minor

Moderato ♩ = 72 (Tovey: similar; maestoso)

45
50
55
60

65
70
75
80
Oder:

Prelude 17, A-flat Major

20
25
30
35

40
45
50
55

60
65
70
75

Fugue 17, A-flat Major

Oder:
30
Oder:
35
40
45
tr
50

Prelude 18, G-sharp Minor

Un poco allegretto ♩ = 80

piano

forte

5

10

15

tr

Oder:

tr

20

Oder:

25
Oder:
30
35
40
Oder:
45
50

Fugue 18, G-sharp Minor

Non troppo allegro ♩. = 76

40
45
50
55
60
65
70

75
80
85
90
95
100
105

110
115
120
125
130
135
140

Prelude 19, A Major

20
25
30

Fugue 19, A Major

Moderato ♩ = 88 (Tovey: faster; allegro)

Prelude 20, A Minor

20
Oder:
25
30

Fugue 20, A Minor

Prelude 21, B-flat Major

25
30
35
Oder:
40
45

50
55
60
65
Oder:

70
75
80
85

Fugue 21, B-flat Major

Allegretto ♩ = 126
(Tovey: similar; in menuetto tempo)

50
55
60
65
70
Oder:
75
80
85
90

Prelude 22, B-flat Minor

Oder:

Fugue 22, B-flat Minor

55
60
65
70
75

Prelude 23, B Major

Oder:
tr
25
30
35
40
45

Fugue 23, B Major

Andante 𝅗𝅥 = 63 *(Tovey: a shade faster)*

a 4.

5

10

15

20

25

30

35
40
45
50
55

60
65
70
75
80

85
90
95
100

Allegro 𝅗𝅥 = 66 *(Tovey: somewhat slower)*

Prelude 24, B Minor

Fugue 24, B Minor

Allegro moderato ♩. = 54

75
80
85
90
95
100